To Carol Anne,
You do, right!
Chandrama Ande

I do
I don't

I Do, I Don't: How to Build a Better Marriage
Chandrama Anderson MA, LMFT
Illustrated by Nur Jaffar G. Latip

Book designed and edited by Woodrow Phoenix

Published by Soaring Penguin Press
12 Lexden Drive
Seaford
East Sussex
BN25 3BD

ISBN 978-1-908030-57-3

Printed in China

Be the first to find out about further developments associated with *I Do I Don't* and other titles and projects coming from Soaring Penguin Press. Sign up for our newsletter at https://www.soaringpenguinpress.com/contact/

I do
I don't

How to build a better marriage

Chandrama Anderson
MA, LMFT

Illustrated by
Nur Jaffar G. Latip

SOARING PENGUIN PRESS

Contents

This book has been printed on paper you can write on. We encourage you, as you use this book, to mark, scribble and highlight things that appeal or occur to you.

You can obtain the free *I Do, I Don't* companion workbook by visiting www.connect2relate.com. The workbook includes the PIIP pages included here, plus additional PIIP content.

Introduction &
How to Use this Book

ALL of us want to be loved, seen, heard and understood. If you don't show up genuinely in your relationship, then who gets loved? Your persona.

I Do, I Don't is useful for and applicable to couples of different/all races, ethnicities, gender and sexual orientations. Everyone needs to work on their relationship, before and after saying, "I do." Here are the tools you need.

Each chapter, and the tools therein, build upon one another. Given that, it's most useful to read from beginning to end. Either:

Read all the way through, and then come back and go chapter by chapter and work on the *Put it Into Practice (PIIP)* sections.

OR

Read one chapter at a time, and work on the *Put it Into Practice* sections.

AND

I highly recommend going through the entire book again and focusing on the art; it's incredible.

However, feel free to jump in anywhere if something catches your eye; you can go back and read the previous chapters afterwards.

I Do, I Don't is full of practical tools that enable you to build a better marriage. The tools are useful in all your relationships, personal and professional. With daily practice, you will gain mastery, and use them in an "unconscious competent" manner.

Clients tell me these tools take time they don't have. I say the time you spend on the front end will save so much time and angst you currently spend upset, seething, or making repairs.

If you're interested in a reading group with me or with peers, check out the 'Options for Working with Chandrama' page.

Cheers to building a better marriage!

– Chandrama

Foreword

IF WE ARE genuinely honest with ourselves and our significant others, we all have had our share of struggles consistently communicating with loved ones without conflicts, misunderstandings, occasional eye rolling and worse, hurt feelings.

Why is that?

Well, we never took a course entitled *Marriage 101* or *Intro to Effectively Communicating Feelings*, that's for sure. In general, we are not well prepared with the tools needed for healthy interpersonal relationships. We have not mastered the basics of effective, emotionally attuned conversations leading to deeper connections and intimacy.

We also do not fully understand how our parents' modeled behaviors have had a lasting impact on us. We carry forward every day the wounds (shame, guilt, insecurities) of our family of origin and "inner child" which negatively impacts those around us and especially those we love most.

As such, there is no wonder why the divorce rate is so high with communications issues cited as one of the most common reasons for divorce, among others.

No doubt we have the greatest intentions each day to emotionally attune to our partners and nurture healthy, mutually rewarding relationships but, we fall short.

Now, scene change. Imagine a marriage manual—in a format that beautifully blends words and graphics—diagnosing real world situations, challenging conversations and relationship disconnects.

Imagine understanding so much more precisely how and why we interact and unknowingly sabotage relationships the ways we do.

And even better, imagine implementing easy to understand, practical tools that will help us all better understand each other's feelings and consistently create more emotionally engaged connections.

Better yet, these tools work with kids, friends, family, and co-workers, too.

In *I Do, I Don't: How to Build a Better Marriage* my former colleague, Chandrama Anderson, shares an innovative methodology, supported by valuable insights, examples and tools drawn from her years of experience as a licensed psychotherapist, enabling couples to enjoy healthier, healing relationships delivering deeper emotional connections and intimacy.

When Chandrama reached out to me to share her latest book, it was a long time since our days disrupting the publishing world and lecturing at Stanford. In reading *I Do, I Don't* I was struck by how she explained a complex topic like relationships and made it so easy to understand using real-world examples and pictorial graphics.

As the founder/CEO of the . . . *For Dummies* brand & book series that has sold over 250 million copies, I have a passion for making learning fun and easy. I could immediately see Chandrama did just that in creating this new format. In

I Do, I Don't the author has delivered a breakthrough comic format expertly explaining a universal topic that continues to challenge millions of couples around the world.

Chandrama has written an easy to understand (and apply) book that weaves together proven couple's counseling and communications tools and psychological education from many disparate sources throughout the history of psychology. She understands that when couples are struggling, each partner wants immediate behavioral change from the other and more emotionally curious conversations, calmer and more compassionate responses and, frankly, more hugs.

I Do, I Don't is presented in an easy-to-grasp and immediately useful format—a graphic novelization of a couple relationship, including disconnects, healing, and new tools for better communication and intimacy—to show couples experiencing marital and relationship difficulties how to quickly get back on track.

I believe this is the first in a long line of books from Chandrama using this format and here is the reason why. According to the National Institute of Health, "the combined language of words and pictures that is the comic medium gives approachability and emotional impact to these personal stories, and even to the clinical data they sometimes include." Chandrama's mission in creating this book of art is to help couples worldwide—despite issues such as access, affordability, or social/cultural stigmas—to seeking therapy. *I Do, I Don't* is the marriage manual and couples/therapist's companion workbook to help support this important mission.

I Do, I Don't also hit home for me. In my own work absorbing books, podcasts, webinars and workshops in my journey to be the best husband, father and friend I can be, I immediately identified with how Chandrama uses a common language of "I feel _____" statements instead of the oft used, accusatory "You" statements as a new coping strategy to express one's feelings more authentically with one's partner. It's a subtle but profound shift in language that will convert difficult conversations that make us feel sad, hurt, or upset into safe, emotionally attuned connections.

I am also a fan of hands-on exercises in books on relationships and in this regard Chandrama shines. Included at the end of each chapter are "Put It Into Practice" worksheets and chapter summaries that guide couples through the core lessons in each chapter and how to thoughtfully and intentionally apply these concepts in their relationship. All couples need to work on their relationship after saying "I do."

Give yourself, your significant other and the most important people in your life the greatest gift—the gift of *I Do, I Don't* and a commitment to do your work to be the best version of your SELF. It will change your life and transform your most important and intimate relationships.

–John Kilcullen

LEGEND

DESPITE THE FACT THAT IT APPEARS THERE ARE ONLY TWO PEOPLE IN YOUR RELATIONSHIP, THE INTERNALIZED VOICES OF YOUR MOTHER, FATHER, AND YOUR UNCONSCIOUS MIGHT BE WREAKING HAVOC IN YOUR RELATIONSHIP, UNBEKNOWNST TO YOU. IN ADDITION TO NURTURE AND NATURE, YOUR PARENTS' VOICES ARE ALIVE IN YOU. THEY INFLUENCE YOUR EMOTIONS, WORDS AND BEHAVIOR. TO ILLUMINATE THIS, MOM'S AND DAD'S VOICES ARE ILLUSTRATED ON THE SHOULDERS OF BEN AND GRACE. SIMILARLY, THE UNCONSCIOUS, WHICH IS THE PART OF THE MIND WHICH IS INACCESSIBLE TO THE CONSCIOUS MIND BUT WHICH AFFECTS BEHAVIOR AND EMOTIONS, IS BROUGHT TO LIGHT IN A RED BUBBLE.

Chapter 1:

Anxious & Uncomfortable

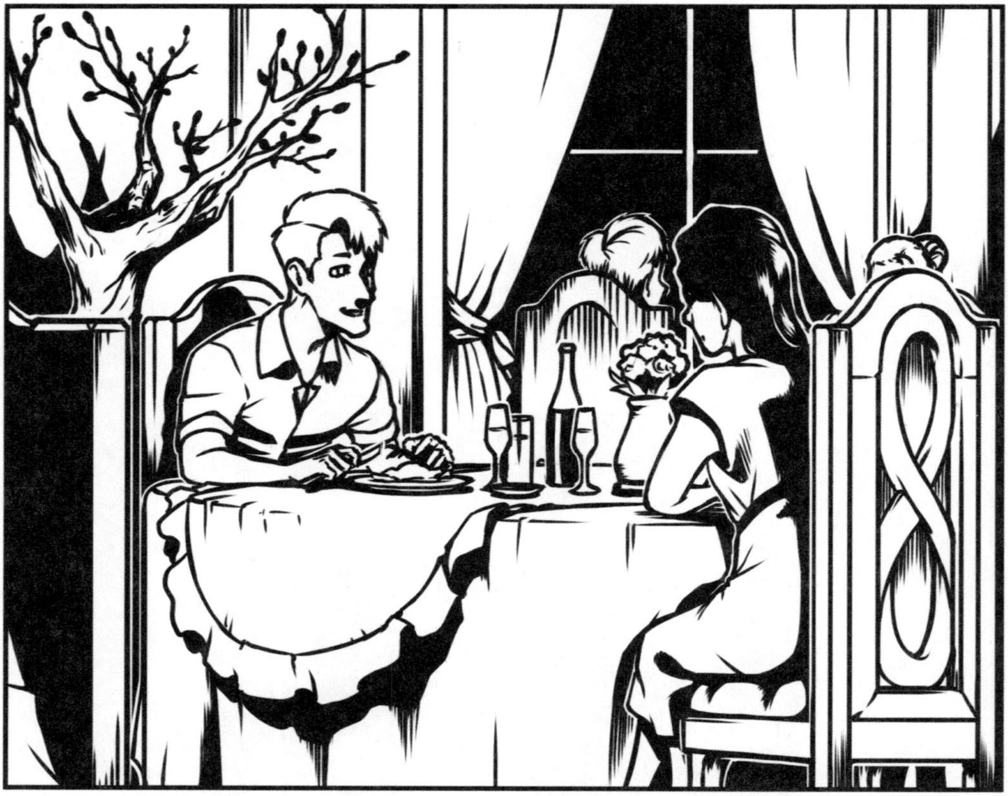

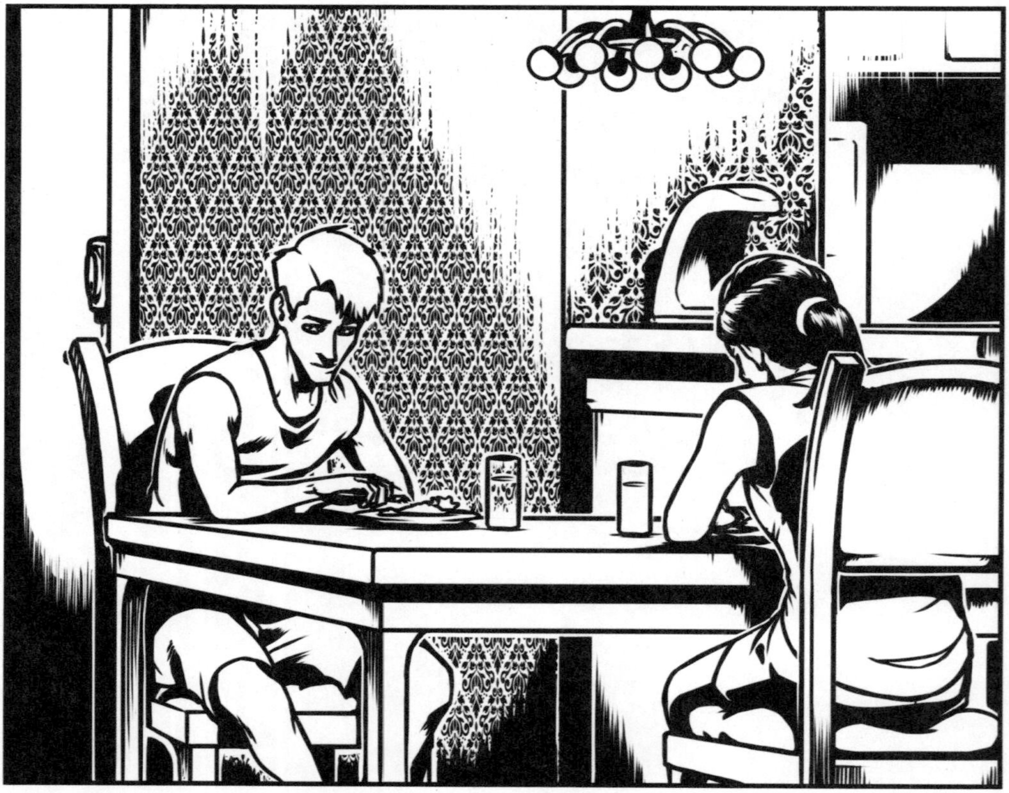

Jo Satlof, MA, MFT
Couples Counseling

COME IN AND TAKE A SEAT.

HI GRACE. HI BEN. I'M JO.

PLEASE TELL ME WHY YOU'RE HERE AND WHAT YOUR GOALS ARE.

WE GET ALONG FINE. BUT WE LIVE LIKE ROOMMATES.

WE BARELY HAVE SEX.

THE THIRD BRAIN TO DEVELOP IS THE CORTICAL OR THINKING/RESPONDING BRAIN. IT TAKES A LOT MORE ENERGY, AND IS THEREFORE SLOWER TO COME ONLINE.

SO YOU HAVE AN INTERACTION THAT TRIGGERS YOU (LIMBIC, 1/200th OF A SECOND) AND YOUR FIRST IMPULSE IS TO REACT. YOU NEED TO WAIT, MEANING ZIP YOUR LIPS, UNTIL YOU CAN RESPOND (CORTICAL BRAIN).

DOES THAT MAKE SENSE?

YES.

ANY QUESTIONS SO FAR?

NO.

YOU TWO JUST HAD AN EMOTIONAL TRIGGER. NO JUDGEMENT HERE; JUST WONDERING WHICH COPING STRATEGY YOU EACH USE.

GRACE, DID YOU WANT TO FIGHT, FLEE OR FREEZE?

BEN, WHAT ABOUT YOU?

I THINK I FIGHT; OTHERWISE FLEE.

I FLEE OR FREEZE.

GRACE, IF YOU FIGHT, BEN WILL RETREAT MORE. WHEN HE RETREATS, YOU COME TOWARD HIM MORE, RIGHT?

THIS IS A VERY COMMON PATTERN COUPLES GET INTO AND CAN BE CHANGED.

HERE'S A TOOL: TRAFFIC LIGHTS. GREEN MEANS YOU'RE CALM, CAN LISTEN AND YOU'RE OPEN TO EACH OTHER'S INPUT AND INFLUENCE.

YELLOW MEANS YOU'RE STARTING TO GET TRIGGERED. RED MEANS YOU'RE BASICALLY SEEING RED AND NOTHING PRODUCTIVE WILL COME OF CONTINUING A CONVERSATION.

IN FACT, IT IS LIKELY THINGS WILL FURTHER ESCALATE INTO A DISAGREEMENT OR ARGUMENT.

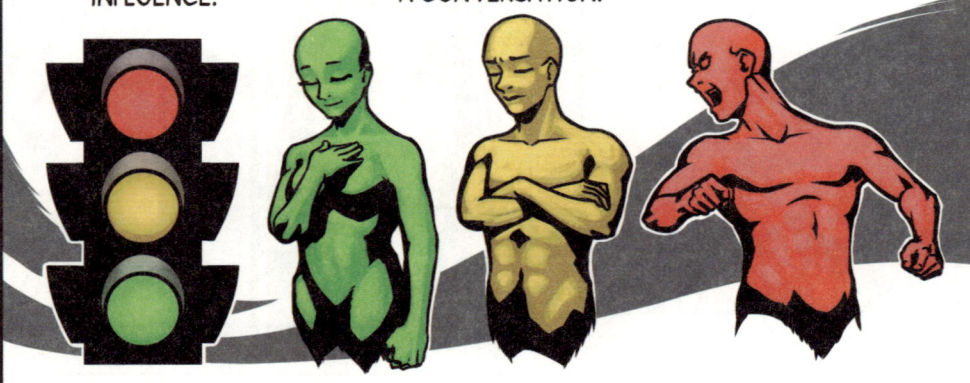

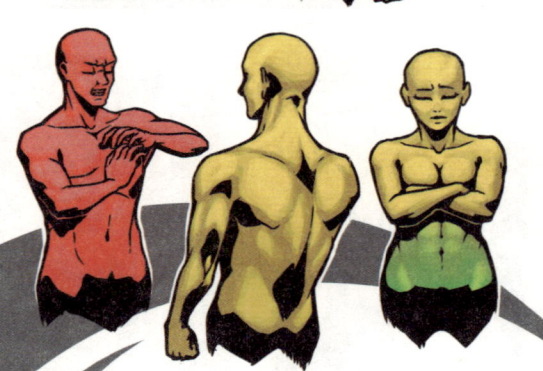

I ONLY WANT YOU TO TALK ABOUT CONTENT WHEN YOU'RE GREEN. IF YOU'RE RED, GIVE A HAND SIGNAL FOR A TIME OUT AND TAKE 30 MINUTES TO PHYSIOLOGICALLY RECOVER.

IF YOU'RE THE ONE THAT'S RED, IT'S YOUR RESPONSIBILITY TO COME BACK TO THE OTHER. IF YOU'RE YELLOW, SWITCH FROM CONTENT TO PROCESS.

TOO BAD NO ONE CAN READ EACH OTHER'S MIND. YOU'RE GOING TO HAVE TO TALK TO EACH OTHER. WE'LL WORK ON IT HERE.

OKAY, TAKE A DEEP BREATH, BEN. LOOK AT GRACE AND GIVE HER AN ANSWER.

SIGH

I DON'T KNOW.

NO ONE COMFORTED ME.

DO YOU KNOW HOW TO COMFORT BEN?

NOT REALLY.

VULNERABLE.

WHAT IS IT YOU KNOW ABOUT BEN NOT KNOWING HOW HE NEEDS TO BE COMFORTED.

I THINK HIS PARENTS FOUGHT A LOT AND IT WAS TENSE IN HIS HOUSE GROWING UP.

GRACE, ASK HIM IF THERE'S A GRAIN OF TRUTH IN THAT.

HONEY, IS THERE A GRAIN OF TRUTH TO THAT?

YEAH. BUT THAT DOESN'T MATTER NOW.

I'LL COME BACK TO THAT COMMENT LATER.

BEN, TELL GRACE ONE SMALL THING YOU NEED RIGHT NOW.

A HUG, I GUESS.

OKAY, STAND UP, AND HUG EACH OTHER FOR TWO MINUTES. MAKE SURE YOUR BELLIES ARE FULLY TOUCHING.

I'LL TIME YOU.

. . .

CHECK IN AND ASK EACH OTHER WHAT COLOR YOU ARE NOW.

PUT IT INTO PRACTICE

THREE BRAINS

Agree that you're going to notice and say aloud when you:

- React, instead of respond.
- Respond.
- Want to fight, flee, or freeze.

TRAFFIC LIGHTS ●●●

Notice what color you are, and ask your partner. If you're red, take 30 minutes to self-soothe and calm your physiology, then return to your partner. Always switch to process from content if you're not green.

30 MINUTES

COMFORT

Figure out what comforts each of you and practice comforting in ways your partner specified (even if you're uncomfortable).

CONTENT VS. PROCESS

Content is any topic. Process is feelings, wants, needs, and reactions to content.

CONTENT

PROCESS

WHAT COMFORTS YOU?

Put a checkmark by what comforts you. Share this with your partner.
Notice when you need comfort. Do you generally self-soothe, or do you turn to
each other for comfort? Practice comforting one another.

DOING/ACTIVITY

Playing an instrument

Exercising

Yoga/Stretching/Running/Walking

Walking meditation

Playing with your dog/cat

Taking a nap

Taking photos

Talking to a friend

Singing/Dancing

Playing a game

Touching (handholding, bodywork)

Sex

Working on a project

Creating/Writing/Drawing

Knitting/Sewing/Crocheting

Baking/Cooking

Planning an adventure

Going for a drive

Riding your bike/motorcycle/horse

BEING/QUIET

Listening to music

Taking a bath or hot tub

Getting out into nature

Meditating

Having a cup of tea or coffee

Heavy blanket

Reading

Having a cool drink in a beautiful place

Watching TV or a movie

Sitting in a quiet place

Cloud gazing

Hanging out at a cafè

Being near a body of water

ADD WHAT COMFORTS YOU:

PUT IT INTO PRACTICE

GOALS

Your goal throughout the book (and in your life overall) is to integrate your emotional reactions with your cortical, thinking processes. This allows you to *respond* with an even keel, instead of *reacting*, which often leads to strife. Combining your emotional life and thinking brain leads to an emotionally healthy and connected relationship.

Give each other privacy to think and respond; each use your own pages, (or request the free *I Do, I Don't* companion workbook from www.connect2relate.com). Then discuss and share with each other. You're not required to share everything. However, ask yourself about what you don't want to reveal with your partner.

TRAFFIC LIGHTS ● ● ●

Look at page 22 to view Traffic Lights.

- Now, on page 12 circle what color Traffic Lights Ben and Grace are in panel 1.   **GREEN**   **YELLOW**   **RED**

- What color are they in panel 2?   **GREEN**   **YELLOW**   **RED**

- Generally, what color Traffic Light are you at home?   **GREEN**   **YELLOW**   **RED**

- At work?   **GREEN**   **YELLOW**   **RED**

- With your family of origin? (the people you grew up with)   **GREEN**   **YELLOW**   **RED**

- With your friends?   **GREEN**   **YELLOW**   **RED**

Go to page 22:
- What does Green light mean?

- What does Yellow light mean?

- What does Red light mean?

PUT IT INTO PRACTICE

FIGHT/FLEE/FREEZE

See page 21. When you're triggered, or flooded with emotions, which is your F-mode? Fight, flee, or freeze?

If you've noticed, what F-mode your partner tends to go to when upset?

Share and discuss.

CONTENT VS. PROCESS

Look at page 23, Content/Process.
What is Content?

What is Process?

Briefly describe a recent time you were stuck in Content. What was the Content?

How did it go between you?

COMFORT

Look at the Comfort list and circle what comforts you, and put a check by what comforts your partner. Share your lists, compare, and educate one another.

PUT IT INTO PRACTICE

TAKEAWAYS

Takeaways are what was learned and/or understood in a chapter.

• What are Grace's takeaways from Chapter 1?

• What are Ben's takeaways from Chapter 1?

• What are your takeaways from Chapter 1?

HOMEWORK

YOUR HOMEWORK THIS WEEK IS TO CHECK IN REGULARLY AS TO WHAT COLOR YOU ARE, AND ONLY TO TALK ABOUT CONTENT WHEN YOU'RE GREEN.

ALSO WORK ON FINDING OUT WHAT YOU EACH NEED TO BE COMFORTED.

Chapter 2:

How Attached Are You?

ONE NIGHT I TOLD YOU I WANTED TO PLAY VIDEO GAMES FOR AN HOUR.

AND AFTERWARD I HUNG OUT WITH YOU.

BEN, ASK GRACE HOW THAT FELT.

IT WAS GREAT!

HAHAHA. GRACE, HOW DID THAT FEEL?

YOU FINALLY GOT OFF THAT DAMN PHONE!

THAT'S A THOUGHT. START WITH "I FELT..."

MAN, THIS IS HARD WORK.

I FELT I MATTERED TO YOU.

HOW DO YOU THINK BEN FELT HEARING THE TWO DIFFERENT STATEMENTS?

ANTAGONIZED. THE OTHER COULD CREATE CONNECTION.

BEN, WHAT DO YOU THINK?

THE PREMISE THAT RELATES TO YOU AS A COUPLE IS THAT THE "SECURE BOND" YOU NEEDED AS CHILDREN WITH YOUR MOM IS SOUGHT — AND NEEDED — AGAIN WITH YOUR PARTNER.

THIS IS AN EVOLUTIONARY, BIOLOGICAL DRIVE FOR CONNECTION THAT AFFECTS YOUR BRAIN MAKE-UP.

FUNDAMENTALLY: ARE YOU THERE FOR ME? DO YOU HAVE MY BACK? CAN I COUNT ON YOU?

AS A CHILD, IF YOU RECEIVED CONSISTENT, LOVING AND DEPENDABLE CARE, IT LEADS TO SECURE ATTACHMENT. IN OTHER WORDS, *GOOD ENOUGH PARENTING;* NOT PERFECT.

IF MOM WAS UNRELIABLE, DISMISSIVE, OR DEROGATORY, OR SHE WAS INCONSISTENT IN BEING LOVING AND SUPPORTIVE, THAT LEADS TO ANXIOUS OR AVOIDANT ATTACHMENT. AN "ISLAND."

THIS RINGS A BELL.

IF YOU WERE OFTEN IGNORED OR SHE WAS PREOCCUPIED, IT LEADS TO ANXIETY EXPRESSED AS ANGRY OR RESISTANT ATTACHMENT. A "WAVE."

Hmm.

LOOK AT EACH OTHERS' FACES AND BODY LANGUAGE. WHAT DO YOU NOTICE?

GRACE LOOKS ANGRY.

DON'T INTERPRET YET. JUST SAY WHAT YOU SEE.

SHE LOOKS ANGRY. I'VE SEEN IT A MILLION TIMES.

43

AND WHEN THEY DID PAY ATTENTION, THEY PUSHED GRACE.

ASK GRACE IF THIS IS CORRECT.

IS THIS YOUR EXPERIENCE GROWING UP?

YES! I DIDN'T KNOW YOU SAW IT SO CLEARLY.

SHARE HOW YOU'RE EACH FEELING RIGHT NOW.

I FEEL RELIEVED AND SAD,

HE GETS IT, AND I'M SAD THAT I GREW UP THIS WAY.

I FEEL GLAD WE'RE TALKING ABOUT IT.

I'M UNCERTAIN WHERE THIS IS GOING. WILL THIS MAKE HER CHANGE?

BEN, ASK GRACE IF SHE NEEDS ANYTHING FROM YOU BEFORE WE GET BACK TO ATTACHMENT THEORY.

DO YOU?

45

I'M OKAY FOR NOW

MAKE EYE CONTACT FOR A BIT, AND TAKE A FEW DEEP BREATHS.

Deep breath

Hahaha

Hahaha

THE REASON ATTACHMENT MATTERS, IS THAT HOWEVER ONE WAS ATTACHED AS A BABY IS LIKELY HOW ONE WILL ATTACH WITH AN ADULT PARTNER.

UWAAH
WAAH

WILL YOU LET YOURSELF BE LOVED AND COMFORTED? ANCHOR.

I WONDER WHAT THAT WOULD BE LIKE?

WILL YOU LACK TRUST THAT YOUR PARTNER WILL BE LOVING AND COMFORTING CONSISTENTLY, LEAVING YOU WONDERING WHAT YOU'LL GET IN ANY GIVEN INTERACTION? ISLAND.

MUST SUCK FOR BEN.

WILL YOU EXPECT THAT YOU CANNOT COUNT ON ANYONE,

SO THAT EVEN IF YOU'RE IN A RELATIONSHIP, YOU HAVE TO DO EVERYTHING YOURSELF, AND PART OF YOU IS HOLDING BACK? WAVE.

THAT'S WHAT I HAD. I DON'T DO THAT TO BEN —

DO I?

OF COURSE I DO.

49

51

I WANT TO INTRODUCE YOU TO A SCIENTIFIC CONCEPT CALLED NEUROPLASTICITY.

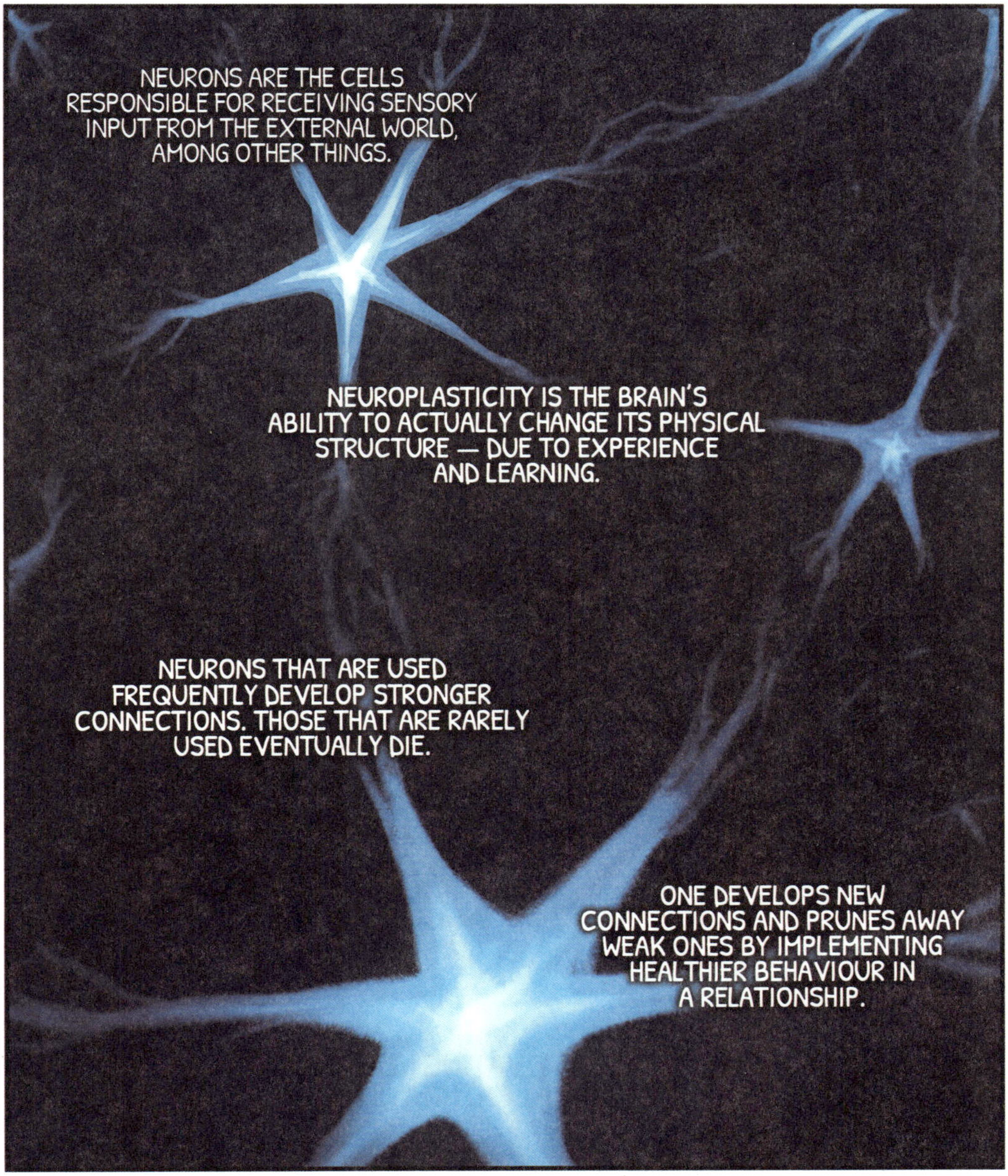

NEURONS ARE THE CELLS RESPONSIBLE FOR RECEIVING SENSORY INPUT FROM THE EXTERNAL WORLD, AMONG OTHER THINGS.

NEUROPLASTICITY IS THE BRAIN'S ABILITY TO ACTUALLY CHANGE ITS PHYSICAL STRUCTURE — DUE TO EXPERIENCE AND LEARNING.

NEURONS THAT ARE USED FREQUENTLY DEVELOP STRONGER CONNECTIONS. THOSE THAT ARE RARELY USED EVENTUALLY DIE.

ONE DEVELOPS NEW CONNECTIONS AND PRUNES AWAY WEAK ONES BY IMPLEMENTING HEALTHIER BEHAVIOUR IN A RELATIONSHIP.

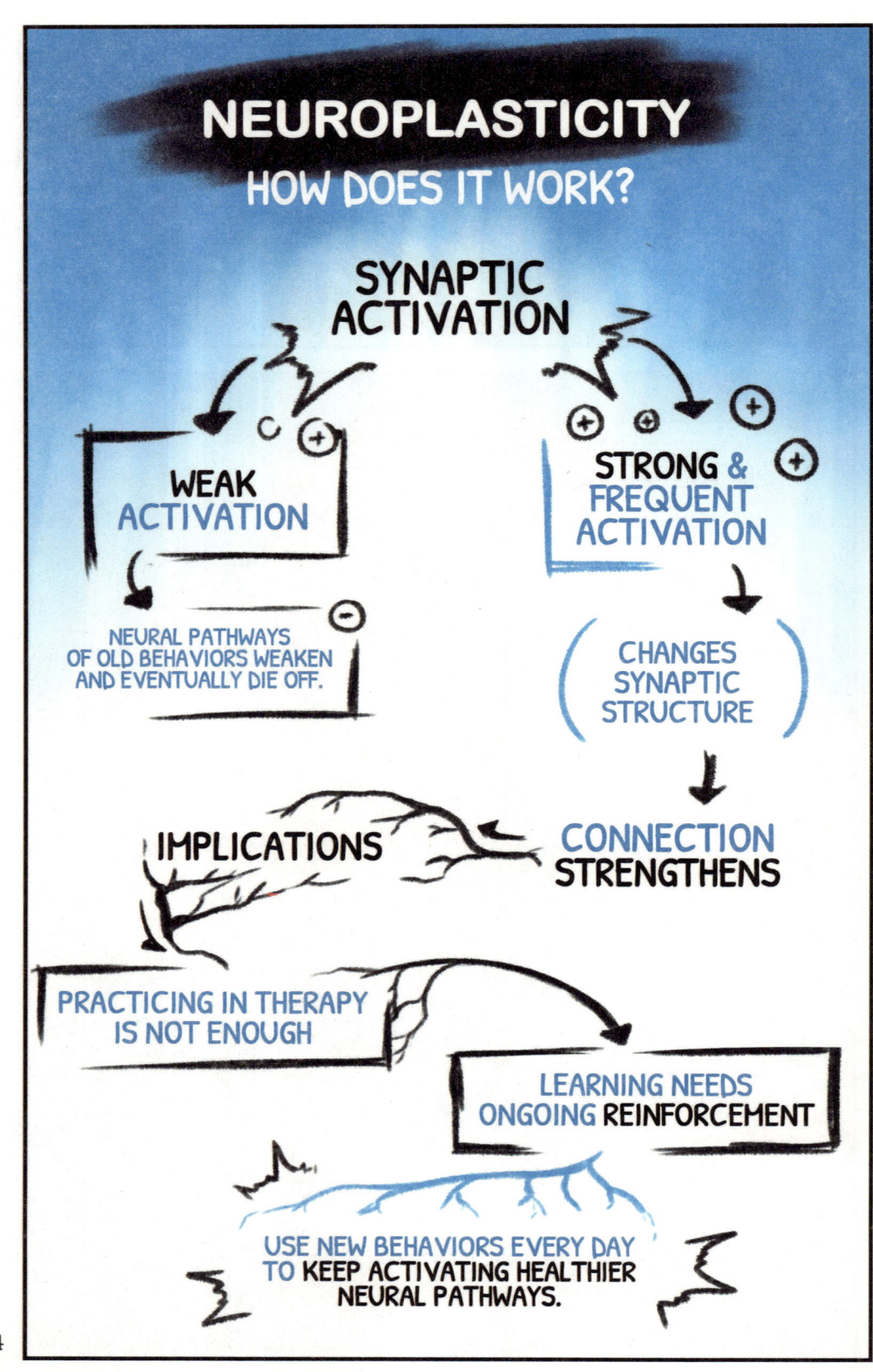

NEUROPLASTICITY
HOW DOES IT WORK?

SYNAPTIC ACTIVATION

WEAK ACTIVATION

STRONG & FREQUENT ACTIVATION

NEURAL PATHWAYS OF OLD BEHAVIORS WEAKEN AND EVENTUALLY DIE OFF.

CHANGES SYNAPTIC STRUCTURE

IMPLICATIONS

CONNECTION STRENGTHENS

PRACTICING IN THERAPY IS NOT ENOUGH

LEARNING NEEDS ONGOING REINFORCEMENT

USE NEW BEHAVIORS EVERY DAY TO KEEP ACTIVATING HEALTHIER NEURAL PATHWAYS.

SIMPLY, NEUROPLASTICITY MEANS YOUR BRAIN CAN CHANGE OVER TIME, AS YOU BEHAVE DIFFERENTLY, AND MOVE TOWARD SECURE ATTACHMENT.

THERE'S A SAYING: "NEURONS THAT FIRE TOGETHER WIRE TOGETHER."

WHEN YOU ACT OR THINK IN NEW, HEALTHIER WAYS, YOU'RE CREATING "ANCHOR" NEURAL PATHWAYS.

YOUR CHILDHOOD COPING SKILLS WERE CRITICAL, AND I HONOR THE WAYS YOU WERE ABLE TO MAKE DO.

HOWEVER, CHILD COPING SKILLS IN AN ADULT RELATIONSHIP USUALLY DON'T WORK OUT WELL.

GUESS NOT, BUT I HATE CHANGE.

SAFETY?

THIS WILL BE AN AREA TO WORK ON AND GROW INTO ADULT STRATEGIES.

SURE DIDN'T HAVE ANY EXAMPLES.

YOU WILL ADD NEW TOOLS TO YOUR TOOLBOX.

HOW TO BUILD A BETTER MARRIAGE

THIS MAKES SENSE. BUT HOW?

I HOPE I CAN DO THIS. I WANT TO, FOR BOTH OF US.

WAVES AND ISLANDS END UP TOGETHER ALL THE TIME. IT IS VERY HARD TO UNDERSTAND WHY S/HE IS MAKING A FUSS, STARTING AN ARGUMENT, OR S/HE KEEPS COMING AT ME WHEN ALL I WANT TO DO IS BE ALONE AND REGROUP.

THOUGHT WE WERE THE ONLY ONES.

I CAN RELATE TO THAT. HAHA.

YOU CAN LEARN TO FUNCTION AS ANCHORS; TO STEP BACK AND SEE YOUR BELOVED *ACTING* AS A WAVE OR ISLAND.

YOUR ATTACHMENT STYLE IS A RESULT OF YOUR UPBRINGING. THE POINT ISN'T TO BLAME PARENTS, BUT TO UNDERSTAND.

INSTEAD OF INTERPRETING BEHAVIORS AS, "YOU ARE DOING THIS OR THAT **TO ME**," YOU CAN WITNESS OLD COPING STRATEGIES.

YOU CAN GAIN COMPASSION, AND STOP REACTING. USE THE CORTICAL BRAIN TO RESPOND.

SHE MAKES IT SOUND SO EASY.

AND SO THE HEALING PROCESS BEGINS. YOU ARE THE LUCKY ONES TO HELP HEAL EACH OTHER'S BAGGAGE.

LET'S LOOK AT YOUR ATTACHMENT STYLE ON THE GRAPH.

WHO WANTS TO GO FIRST?

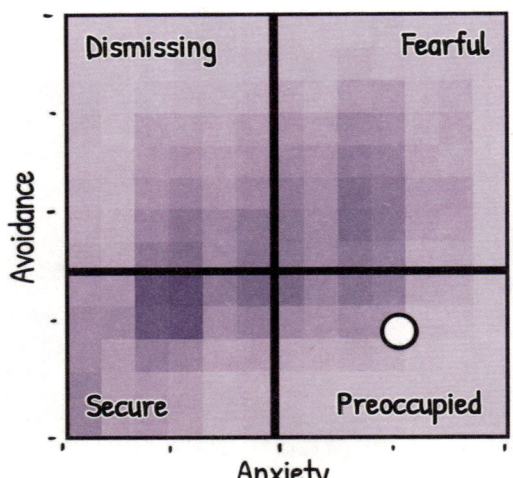

GENERAL ATTACHMENT

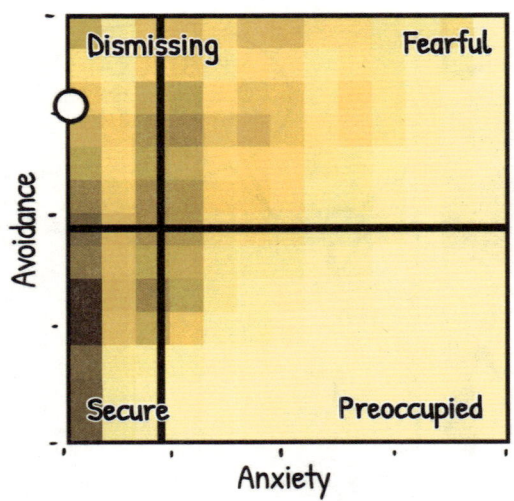

MOM ATTACHMENT

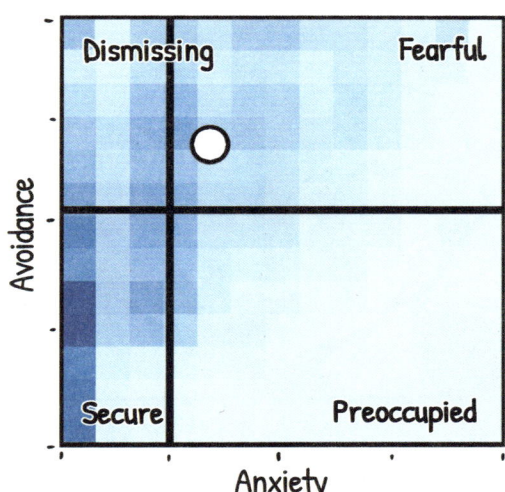

DAD
ATTACHMENT

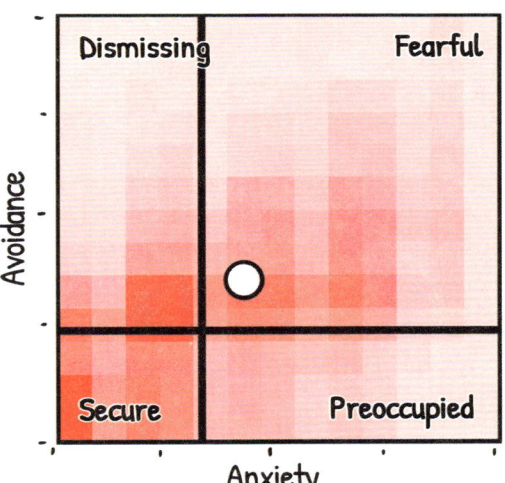

ROMANTIC
ATTACHMENT

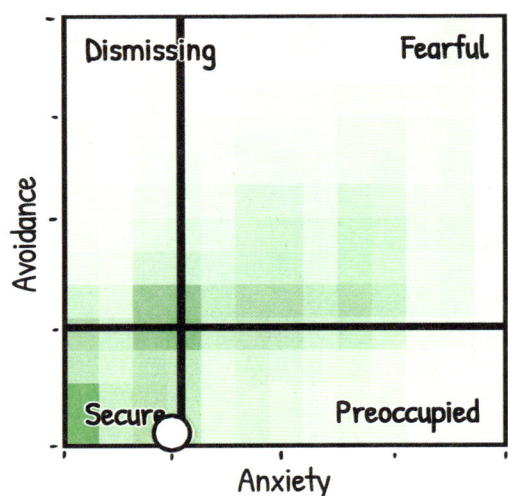

FRIEND
ATTACHMENT

SIT WITH YOUR FEELINGS, EVEN THOUGH IT'S UNCOMFORTABLE.

I see why I avoid Grace.

This is killing me.

YOU DON'T AVOID ME ALL THE TIME.

WHEN YOU'RE STRESSED OR UPSET YOU GO INTO ISLAND MODE

GRACE MAKES A GOOD POINT: WHEN YOU'RE FLOODED, YOU BECOME AN ISLAND.

HOW MUCH OF YOUR TIME DO YOU THINK YOU SPEND AS AN ISLAND?

I'M NOT SURE. HALF?

NOT THAT MUCH.

THE GOAL IS TO BETTER UNDERSTAND YOURSELF AND EACH OTHER. YOU GET TO CHOOSE HOW TO BEHAVE, TO RESPOND. YOU CAN WORK ON NOT REACTING.

THIS IS A LOT TO DIGEST.

THERE'S NO HURRY. OVER THE NEXT WEEK, NOTICE HOW YOU'RE FEELING AND WHAT THOUGHTS ARISE AS YOU DIGEST IT.

PULL

HUG

...

63

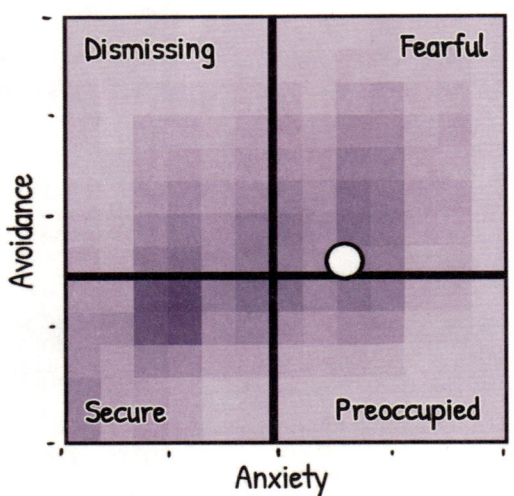

GENERAL ATTACHMENT

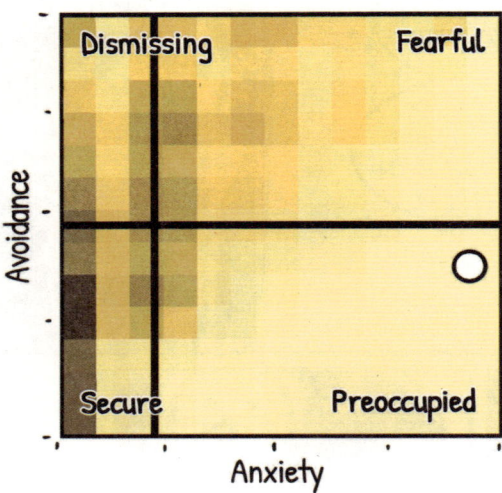

MOM ATTACHMENT

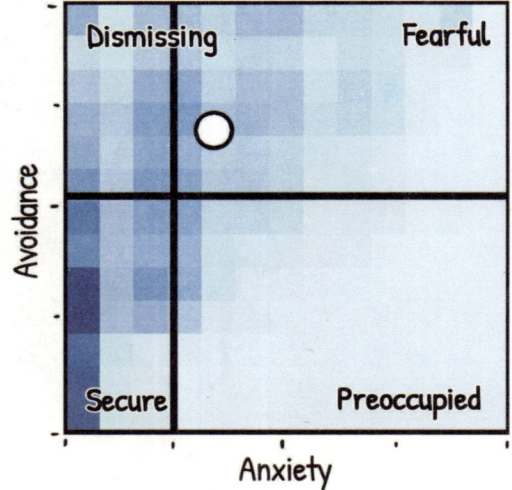

DAD ATTACHMENT

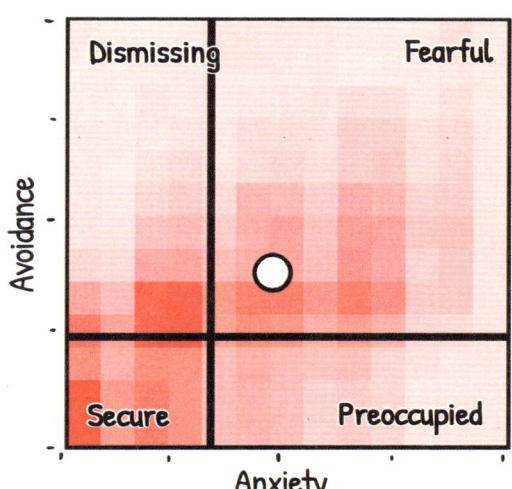

ROMANTIC
ATTACHMENT

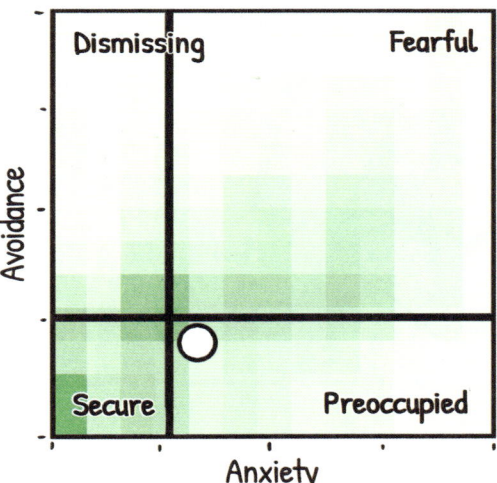

FRIEND
ATTACHMENT

WHY DID OUR PARENTS TREAT US LIKE THEY DID?

USUALLY PARENTS DO THE BEST THEY CAN, GIVEN HOW THEY WERE BROUGHT UP. BEHAVIOR PASSES DOWN THROUGH GENERATIONS UNTIL SOMEONE SAYS,

"ENOUGH! THIS STOPS HERE."

BY BEING HERE, DOING THIS WORK, YOU CALLED "ENOUGH."

BUILD COMPASSION FOR EACH OTHER—AND YOURSELVES.

PUT IT INTO PRACTICE

ATTACHMENT THEORY

Take the quiz at:
http://www.web-research-design.net/cgi-bin/crq/crq.pl

On YouTube, watch:
"The Strange Situation"
and
"Still Face"

SECURE FUNCTIONING = "WE COME FIRST"

1. Give attunement (deep listening and empathy) and be experts about each other.

2. We have each other's backs; we're each the "go to" person.

3. Seek comfort and sex from one another.

4. Create a home that is your haven. Magnify positives and make repairs promptly.

5. Help address distress with eye-to-eye communication and touch.

6. Use attraction to influence each other (not guilt, threat, fear, or shame).

7. Protect your marriage privately and publicly.

8. Be transparent, communicative, and respectful.

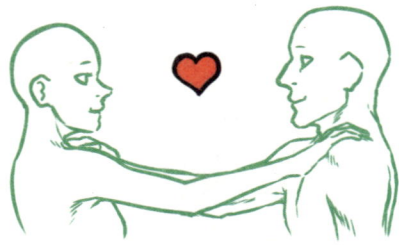

TAKEAWAYS

- On page 36: You only have control over your own behavior. Only police:

  Yourself   Each other

- See pages 38-40: What is the definition of Attachment Theory?

  Lasting connectedness   Have my back   There for me

  I can count on you   All of those

- When you are stressed or emotionally flooded, are you an Anchor, Island or Wave?

- On page 48, panels 3-5: What does Jo say that offers hope?

  Live and behave in new ways   It's a daily choice

  Focus on your hopes for your relationship   All of these

- Starting on page 53: What is neuroplasticity?

  Less used neuropathways weaken   Your brain can change all your life

  The brain changes by employing different behavior   All of these

---

- Review page 58: What's Ben's attachment style in general?

  What's Ben's attachment style with Grace?

- Review page 64: What's Grace's attachment style in general?

  What's Grace's attachment style with Ben?

- See page 66, panel 4: Jo describes intergenerational trauma as:

- What are Grace's takeaways from Chapter 2?

- What are Ben's takeaways from Chapter 2?

PUT IT INTO PRACTICE

TAKEAWAYS

- What are your takeaways from Chapter 2?

HOMEWORK

YOUR HOMEWORK IS TO WATCH "THE STRANGE SITUATION" AND "STILL FACE" ON YOUTUBE, USE TRAFFIC LIGHTS, AND COMFORT EACH OTHER.

Chapter 3:

Using a Personal Weather Report

I wish I was your dog...

WHAT DID YOU EACH DO THIS WEEK TO MAKE YOUR MARRIAGE BETTER?

IT WAS A ROUGH WEEK. TRYING TO DIGEST BEING AN ISLAND, AND WHY.

I'M ANGRY.

75

76

79

81

83

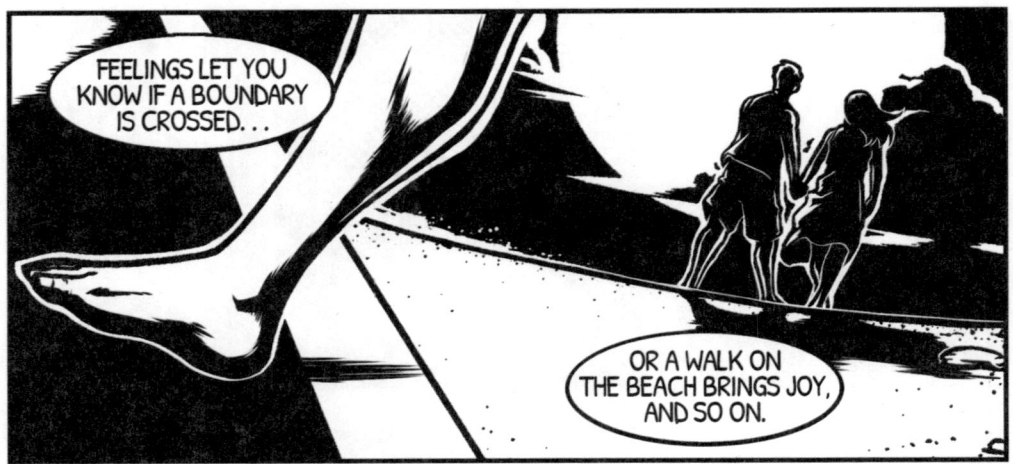

FEELINGS LET YOU KNOW IF A BOUNDARY IS CROSSED. . .

OR A WALK ON THE BEACH BRINGS JOY, AND SO ON.

SHOWING FEELINGS LEADS TO PAIN.

OR . . . CONNECTION?

SHARING FEELINGS CAN BE PAINFUL; AND IMPORTANT. YOU'LL NOT ONLY SURVIVE, BUT BE CLOSER AS YOU GO THROUGH WHATEVER IT IS—TOGETHER.

MOST CHILDREN ARE NOT TAUGHT THE LANGUAGE OF FEELINGS; INSTEAD YOU FOLLOW THE EXAMPLE OF YOUR PARENTS.

Damn skippy!

WHILE THAT MIGHT NOT BE HEALTHY IN AN ADULT RELATIONSHIP, IT FEELS NORMAL.

NOT TALKING

HIGH EXPECTATIONS

OVERBEARING NEGLECTFUL

SHARING FEELINGS WILL LIKELY FEEL FORCED AND ABNORMAL. THAT'S OKAY. YOU'RE CREATING NEW NEURAL PATHWAYS IN YOUR BRAIN.

I THINK I'LL RUIN IT, BUT I'LL TRY.

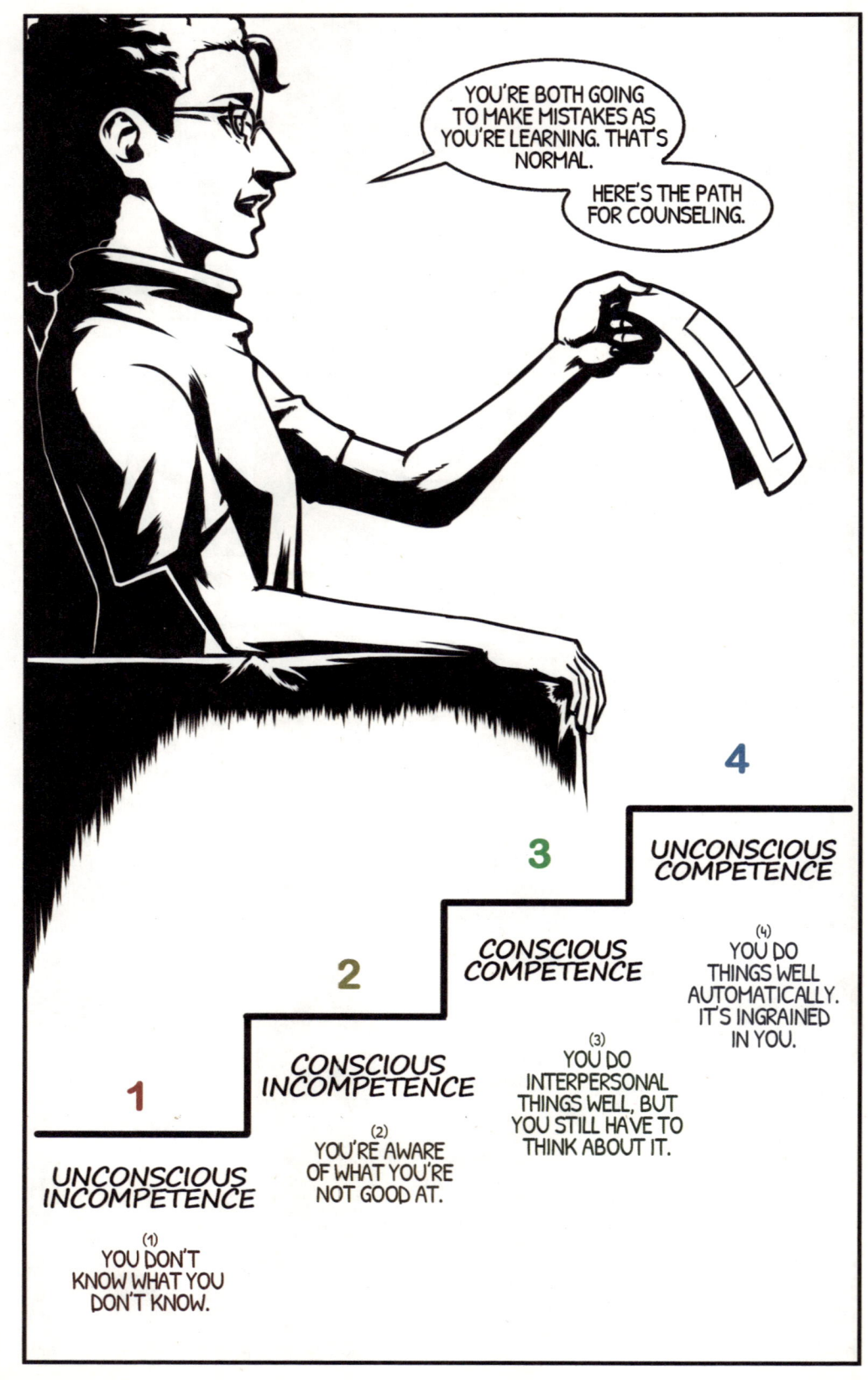

90

TELL ME ABOUT BEING ANNOYED.

I DIDN'T WANT TO TALK ABOUT MY FEELINGS.

I FEEL STUPID AND AMATEURISH.

IT'S ICKY TO FEEL STUPID. WE'RE IN THE SAME BOAT, HONEY.

THAT WAS GOOD ATTUNEMENT, GRACE. YOU LISTENED, ACKNOWLEDGED BEN'S FEELINGS, AND OFFERED EMPATHY.

BEN, LIST GRACE'S FEELINGS AND ASK ABOUT ONE. WE VEERED OFF FOR A BIT, SO IF YOU NEED HELP REMEMBERING, LET GRACE KNOW.

ALSO, BRAINS SPACE OUT 30% OF THE TIME. NO ONE KNOWS WHY. IF YOU MISS WHAT EACH OTHER SAYS, ASK. ANSWER KINDLY.

I WISH I KNEW THAT.

YEAH, IT'S HELPFUL.

YOU FELT WORRIED, EXPOSED, AND . . .

EDGY.

I THINK I UNDERSTAND "EXPOSED," BUT TELL ME.

I DON'T LIKE OPENING UP. I GET SCARED IT WILL BE USED AGAINST ME.

YOUR PARENTS ARE SO MEAN.

MINE TOO.

BEN, TELL GRACE WHAT YOU HEARD HER SAY. CHECK THAT IT'S ACCURATE, AND IF YOU MISSED ANYTHING. THEN GIVE EMPATHY.

SAY, "I HEARD YOU SAY . . ."

I HEARD YOU SAY YOU GET SCARED OPENING UP BECAUSE IT'S BEEN USED AGAINST YOU.

IS THAT RIGHT?

YES.

NERVOUS AND HOPEFUL.

BEN, TRY: "THAT MUST FEEL _____."

THAT MUST BE AWFUL AND MAKE YOU WANT TO HIDE FEELINGS. IS THAT WHY YOU GET MAD AT TIMES?

WOW, BEN. EXACTLY.

HOW DO YOU EACH FEEL RIGHT NOW?

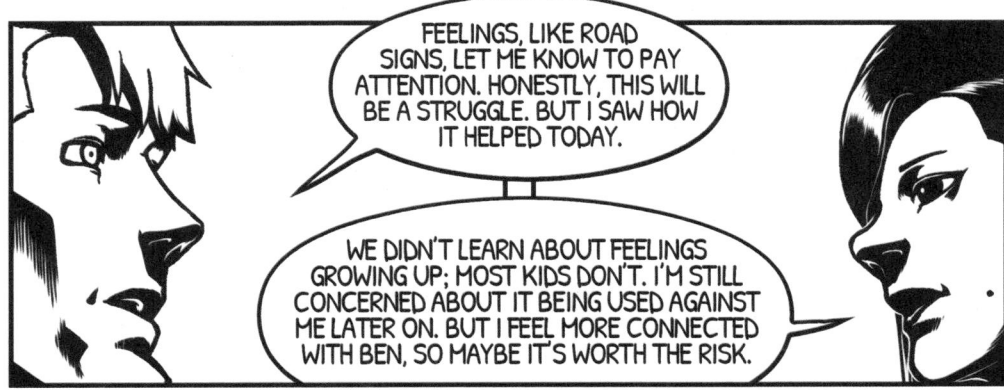

95

I FOUND THE COMPETENCY MAP HELPFUL. I'LL THINK ABOUT MY AUTHENTIC SELF.

I GUESS WE HAVE A LOT SHOVED UNDER THE PROVERBIAL RUG. LEAK OUT REPERCUSSIONS DO HAPPEN.

YOUR HOMEWORK THIS WEEK IS TO DO PERSONAL WEATHER REPORT AT LEAST ONCE A DAY. IF YOU ARE SHORT ON TIME, JUST SHARE THREE FEELINGS. THAT WAY YOU HAVE AN INKLING OF EACH OTHER'S INNER STATES. DO THE LONGER VERSION OF BEING CURIOUS AS OFTEN AS YOU ARE ABLE.

PUT IT INTO PRACTICE

PERSONAL WEATHER REPORT: A snapshot of your internal state

Share three feelings 1-2 times a day, taking turns.

State your partner's feelings and ask for one to be elaborated on.

If you're pressed for time, just share feelings.

WHY FEELINGS MATTER

Sharing feelings leads to being in it together = emotional intimacy.

Feelings let you know there's something to attend to.

Feelings drive actions and behavior, consciously or unconsciously.

WHEN YOU GET INTO IT

Slow down, breathe, get yourself Green.

Use "I" statements, not "You" statements.

Use this formula: When _____ happened, I felt _____, _____,

and a body feeling _____ . What I need/wish for is _____ .

FOUR STAGES OF COMPETENCY

4 Unconscious Competence

3 Conscious Competence

2 Conscious Incompetence

1 Unconscious Incompetence

FEELING LISTS

HAPPY

delighted	transported	light-hearted	vivacious	rapturous
joyful	enthusiastic	buoyant	brisk	high-spirited
festive	inspired	debonair	sparkling	animated
content	glad	bright	merry	frisky
complacent	beatific	free & easy	mirthful	elated
satisfied	pleased	airy	hilarious	exultant
serene	blissful	exuberant	exhilarated	jubilant
comfortable	cheerful	saucy	jovial	
peaceful	genial	jaunty	jolly	
tranquil	cheery	lively	playful	
ecstatic	sunny	spirited	gleeful	

SAD

crestfallen	depressed	somber	oppressed	dejected
despondent	disconsolate	sulky	downhearted	sullen
disheartened	melancholy	joyless	flat	dreadful
discouraged	out of sorts	spiritless	dull	in the dumps
low	heavy-hearted	dismal	gloomy	unhappy
low spirited	disoriented	dark	cheerless	
ill at ease	glum	clouded	woeful	
sorrowful	moody	frowning	woebegone	
downcast	moping	mournful	dreary	

ANGRY

resentful	irritated	enraged	furious	infuriated
annoyed	sullen	sulky	in a stew	irate
inflamed	wrought up	bitter	up in arms	boiling
provoked	worked up	virulent	in a huff	offended
incensed	indignant	acrimonious	wrathful	

HURT

injured	suffering	victimized	tortured	sad
offended	afflicted	heartbroken	piteous	pathetic
grieved	worried	hapless	woeful	tragic
distressed	aching	in despair	rueful	
in pain	crushed	agonized	mournful	

PUT IT INTO PRACTICE

PERSONAL WEATHER REPORT

Got to page 76, panel 6 through page 82. The steps of Personal Weather Report are:

1. Take turns, three feelings, one at a time. Make one a body feeling.
2. Say a feeling you have in this moment.
3. Repeat your partner's three feelings.
4. Ask a question about one of those three feelings (start with anything except 'Why').
5. Say back what you heard your partner answer (not your interpretation or summation).
6. Give empathy; i.e. that must be tough, great, confusing, stressful.
   (Note: giving empathy doesn't mean you agree, it means you care.)
7. Make eye contact to be sure your communication is complete.
8. Switch to your partner's Personal Weather Report and go through steps 1-7.

TAKEAWAYS

- On page 83, panel 6: How are feelings like road signs?

- On pages 85-86: What are several reasons feelings matter?

  Add your reasons:

- On page 86, panel 3: How do you feel as you ask yourself the question about who is you partner supposed to love?

- Here's a big question: What's your mask or persona?

- On page 89, panel 5: Ben asks for a formula to progress in the competency stages. See page 90 for the formula:
  When _____
  _____
  _____

PUT IT INTO PRACTICE

TAKEAWAYS

- Page 91, panel 4: What does attunement consist of?

- On page 95, panels 5–7: What are Ben's and Grace's takeaways from Chapter 3?

- What are your takeaways from Chapter 3?

HOMEWORK

YOUR HOMEWORK THIS WEEK IS TO DO A PERSONAL WEATHER REPORT AT LEAST ONCE A DAY. IF YOU ARE SHORT ON TIME, JUST SHARE THREE FEELINGS. THAT WAY YOU HAVE AN INKLING OF EACH OTHER'S INNER STATES. DO THE LONGER VERSION OF BEING CURIOUS AS OFTEN AS YOU ARE ABLE.

ALSO KEEP UP THE TRAFFIC LIGHTS PRACTICE.

Chapter 4:

Learn Core Tools

103

I'M HUNGRY. I HOPE GRACE HAS BACKED OFF BY NOW.

WE'RE SMART PEOPLE. WHY DO WE DO THIS?

GUESS WE'RE STILL IN PRE-SCHOOL.

STEP BACK FROM CONTENT NOW, AND TELL EACH OTHER ON A PROCESS LEVEL WHAT HAPPENED. GO SLOWLY AND BE TRANSPARENT.

WHAT DOES THAT MEAN?

DID YOU NOTICE HOW QUICKLY YOU BOTH WENT FROM 0-100?

IRONIC

WERE YOU TRANSPARENT ABOUT YOUR FEELINGS, NEEDS, CONCERNS?

TRANSLATE THE CONTENT INTO PROCESS.

I'LL TRY IT. BEN HAS GONE FIRST A FEW TIMES.

I'M STILL WOUND UP THINKING ABOUT IT.

MEMORY ISN'T LIKE A DVD. ONLY EMOTIONAL CONTENT GETS STORED INTO MEMORY—INACCURATELY. IT'S NOT USEFUL TO GET INTO HE SAID/SHE SAID. THAT CAN SPIRAL YOU BACK INTO FAULTY CONTENT.

GRACE STARTED YELLING AT ME THE SECOND I SAW HER!

119

121

"I feel ignored."

"YOU ignore me."

THESE ARE EXAMPLES OF "I" AND "YOU" STATEMENTS.

OH! NOW I GET IT. I FEEL IGNORED; THAT'S AN "I" PROCESS STATEMENT.

AT LEAST WE BOTH GET TO LEARN FROM EACH OTHER'S ATTEMPTS TO SAY THINGS RIGHT.

INSTEAD OF "RIGHT," LET'S SAY "BETTER." WORK ON SHIFTING RIGHT/WRONG TO WHAT HELPS YOU FEEL SEEN AND HEARD.

123

127

PUT IT INTO PRACTICE

DON'T EDITORIALIZE

If you want to be heard, stick with facts.

Yes: I've noticed a lot of work time. I feel ignored.

No: You work all the time and ignore me. You're an asshole!

TRANSPARENCY

No one can read your mind. You have to say what you think, feel, and need.
Don't make your partner excavate.
Part of transparency is context, e.g., "I'm nervous to say this" or
"I feel vulnerable telling you . . ."

SLOW DOWN

Inhale. Exhale. Inhale. Exhale.

Speak slowly, at a reasonable volume and tone.

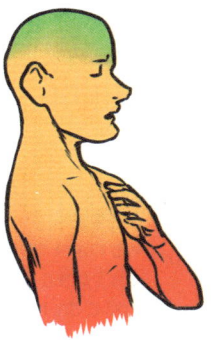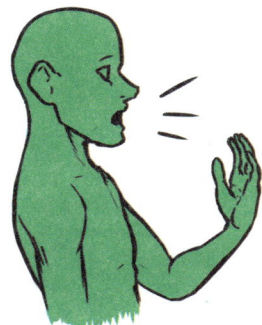

CONTENT VS. PROCESS

Content is defined as the topic of discussion. Process is defined as how you are feeling in the moment about the Content.

Throughout the day, notice when you're in Content or Process. When you're in Content, start paying attention to your Process that's going on underneath.

Generally, when you argue, you are not actually arguing about the topic at hand. You are arguing about not feeling heard, seen or understood. Or perhaps you are feeling sad, hurt, or frustrated. To complicate things further, you may not be aware of the underlying feelings driving the argument.

The solution for arguments is to stop talking about Content. Instead, seek out what's going on in the Process realm. Then, ask, "What do you need from me right now?" Once you're back to Green, you may resume the Content discussion. Never discuss Content when you're Yellow or Red.

Content	Process
How to load the dishwasher.	How I feel when you're telling me how to load the dishwasher.
Who decides our next activity?	Do I feel seen and heard in the decision-making?
How to do a project.	Am I heard and valued as we figure this out?
It's your turn to cook.	Am I stuck in the "fairness" loop?
The kids are leaving messes.	Why am I responsible for everything the kids do? OR I'm not responsible for the kids' messes!
Your driving . . .	I feel anxious/unsafe.
You bought what?!	We can't afford that. OR Money isn't used that way. OR How come you didn't discuss it with me first? OR Are we not on the same page about money after all this time?
Your parents are coming over.	Great, but what are we going to serve? OR I would have liked to have input on that. OR That's stressful. OR I don't want to see them now.

TAKEAWAYS

- On page 106, panels 2-3: Notice how Grace's thoughts shift her from Green Light to Red Light. Don't believe everything you think! What could Grace have said to herself to shift back to Green?

- On page 115: What does Jo want them to be transparent about?

  Concerns   Feelings   Needs   All of them

- On page 116, panel 4: Is memory accurate?   Yes   No

- On page 118: What's editorializing?

- Still on page 118: What do you hear your Mom say in your head?

  What do you hear your Dad say in your head?

- See page 123, panels 1-3: What is transparency?

- Also on page 123, panels 5-6 and page 124: What's the value of slowing down?

- See page 124, panel 3: What's the value of getting to Green Light before talking again?

PUT IT INTO PRACTICE

TAKEAWAYS

- What are Grace's takeaways from Chapter 4?

- What are Ben's takeaways from Chapter 4?

- What are your takeaways from Chapter 4?

HOMEWORK

See page 130: What's Grace's homework?

What's Ben's homework?

Add your homework:

Chapter 5:

HOW TO BUILD A
BETTER MARRIAGE

Cultivate Curiosity

AMY, HOW'S IT GOING?

MATEO AND I ARE THINKING OF TRYING COUPLES COUNSELING.

NOD NOD

GRACE AND I ARE DOING THAT.

EXPOSED.

139

IT'S STILL NEW FOR US. I THINK IT'S HELPING.

IT'S EASIER TO DO WHAT WE'VE ALWAYS DONE; WHAT OUR PARENTS DID. WE'RE TRYING NEW THINGS — WHEN WE REMEMBER.

WE STILL MESS UP. I OFTEN DREAD GOING BUT IT'S WORTH IT.

WHAT'S YOUR HOMEWORK?

WE HAVE TO FIGURE OUT HOW TO COMFORT EACH OTHER.

THOUGHT WE'D KNOW BY NOW. . .

143

OOOH, PDA!

HEY, WE NEED TO TAKE OFF.

GOOD TO SEE ALL OF YOU.

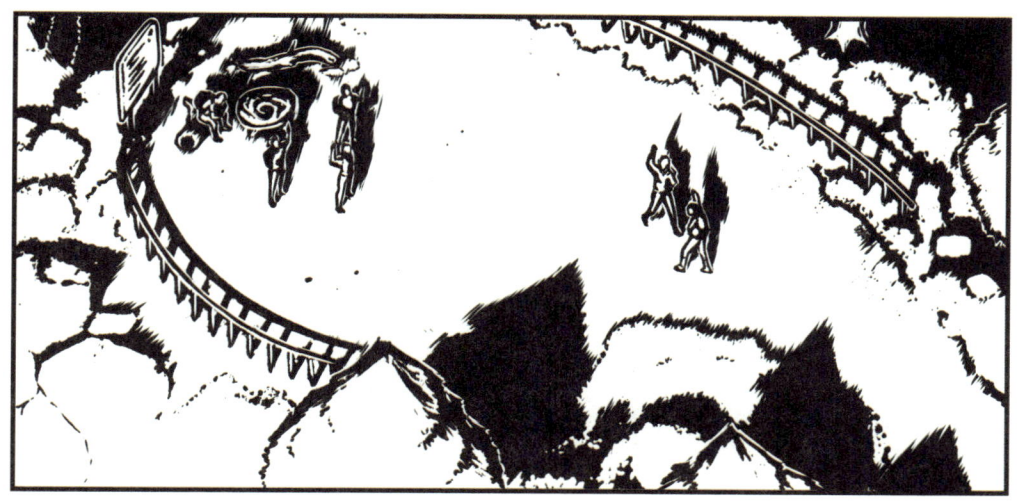

IT'S A LOT MORE THAN THAT!

HANG ON.

I WANT YOU TO OFFER SUGGESTIONS AND DECIDE TOGETHER. DID YOU NOTICE YOU BOTH RAN WITH GRACE'S COMMENT?

FRACTAL SLEEPS BETWEEN US.

NOT ALWAYS!

149

WHAT DOES FRACTAL SLEEPING BETWEEN US MEAN TO YOU?

· · ·

IT DOESN'T MEAN ANYTHING. HE LIKES IT THERE.

NOW WHAT?

TURN

TRY ANOTHER START.

151

WHY IS THIS SUCH A BIG DEAL?

I'M CURIOUS ABOUT YOU SNUGGLING WITH FRACTAL INSTEAD OF ME.

I HAD NO IDEA THIS WAS SUCH A HOTSPOT.

I DON'T KNOW.

ASK HER TO GUESS.

GRACE, MAKE A GUESS.

154

155

157

159

I SAW IT MAKE DAD SMALLER. I WOULD NEVER WANT TO DIMINISH YOU.

MAYBE YOU DON'T THINK YOU'RE DOING IT. I EXPERIENCE IT.

THIS IS REALLY HARD TO SWALLOW. DO I REALLY BOSS GRACE AROUND?

NO! SHE BOSSES ME.

I NEED TO THINK ABOUT THIS, OKAY?

WE'RE ALMOST OUT OF TIME. WE GOT AWAY FROM FRACTAL ON YOUR BED.

YOU CAN CONTINUE THE DISCUSSION ON YOUR OWN OR PICK IT UP NEXT WEEK. NOTICE THAT THE DEEPER ISSUE IS BEN MISSING TOUCH. USUALLY, THE ARGUMENT ISN'T ABOUT THE INITIAL TOPIC.

WE'LL SEE HOW IT GOES.

TAKEAWAYS FROM TODAY?

BE CURIOUS. SHIFT BETWEEN CONTENT AND PROCESS.

SAYING WHAT I HEARD LETS GRACE KNOW I LISTEN TO HER.

WHILE WE DON'T NECESSARILY AGREE, WE CARE.

OKAY. PART OF YOUR HOMEWORK IS TO TAKE THE LOVE LANGUAGE QUIZ. DON'T BE THROWN BY THE QUESTIONS.

DO THE BEST YOU CAN. THE RESULTS ARE ILLUMINATING AND VERY IMPORTANT.

161

CURIOSITY QUESTIONS/STATEMENTS

Tell me more . . .

Say more about that . . .

What does that mean to you?

How are you feeling?

What are you feeling in your body?

I'm curious about . . .

I wonder . . .

What is most important in what you're telling me?

What do you know in yourself about that?

[Repeat back a word or two] You're feeling (happy, sad, angry, hurt).

What does your expression/body posture mean [maybe describe what you see]?

Do you remember other times you felt like this?

What's your earliest memory of this feeling?

What does this remind you of?

Who said that to you in the past?

What else do you remember?

I sense there's something underneath this . . .

Can you go deeper with that . . .

How does that play out between us?

How does that show up in our relationship?

That must be [hard, sad, etc.] . . .

I'm trying to get a felt-sense of that, can you describe it more . . .

How was that for you?

TAKEAWAYS

- On page 146, panel 2: What does Jo want Ben and Grace to do together?

- See page 148, panel 4: Why is Jo asking what number these topics are?

    She's a numbers person   To help them learn with easier topics
          To help Ben and Grace become aware of it

- See page 151, panels 1-2: What happens when Ben goes back to their old communication style?

- Go to page 152, panel 1: What is Ben's content?

    What are his feelings underneath the content—his Process?
          Hurt   Sad   Lonely   Confused   Questioning

- Still on page 152:, panel 4: How does Jo reframe Ben and Grace's behaviours?
         Help them recognize Wave/Island   Steers them to Anchor
         Asks them to think in Secure Functioning   All of these

- See page 154, panel 2: What's the value of going to feelings?
       To stop the argument   Real information is shared   To practice tools

- On page 157, panels 3-4: What does Jo say about repeating and agreeing?

- What are Grace's takeaways from Chapter 5?

PUT IT INTO PRACTICE

TAKEAWAYS

- What are Ben's takeaways from Chapter 5?

- What are your takeaways from Chapter 5?

HOMEWORK

YOUR HOMEWORK THIS WEEK:
TAKE THE 5 LOVE LANGUAGES QUIZ.
PRACTICE BEING CURIOUS. BE TRANSPARENT
ABOUT SHIFTING BETWEEN CONTENT AND
PROCESS. KEEP USING PERSONAL WEATHER
REPORTS AND TRAFFIC LIGHTS.

Chapter 6:

HOW TO BUILD A
BETTER MARRIAGE

Making Use of the Five Love Languages

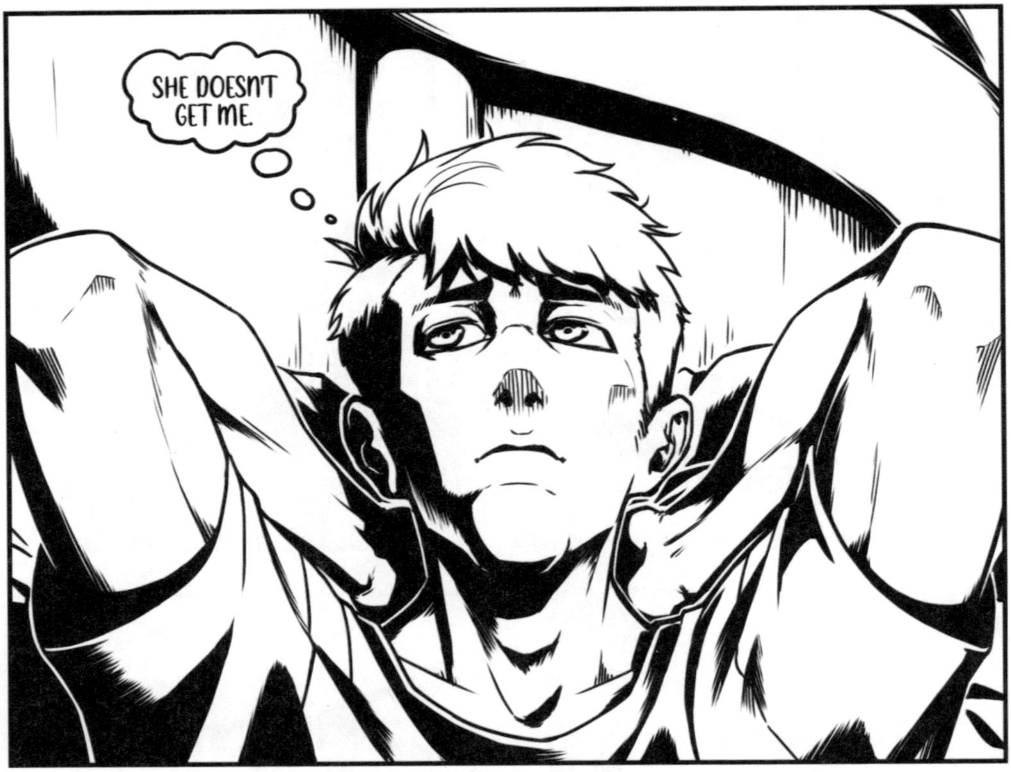
SHE DOESN'T GET ME.

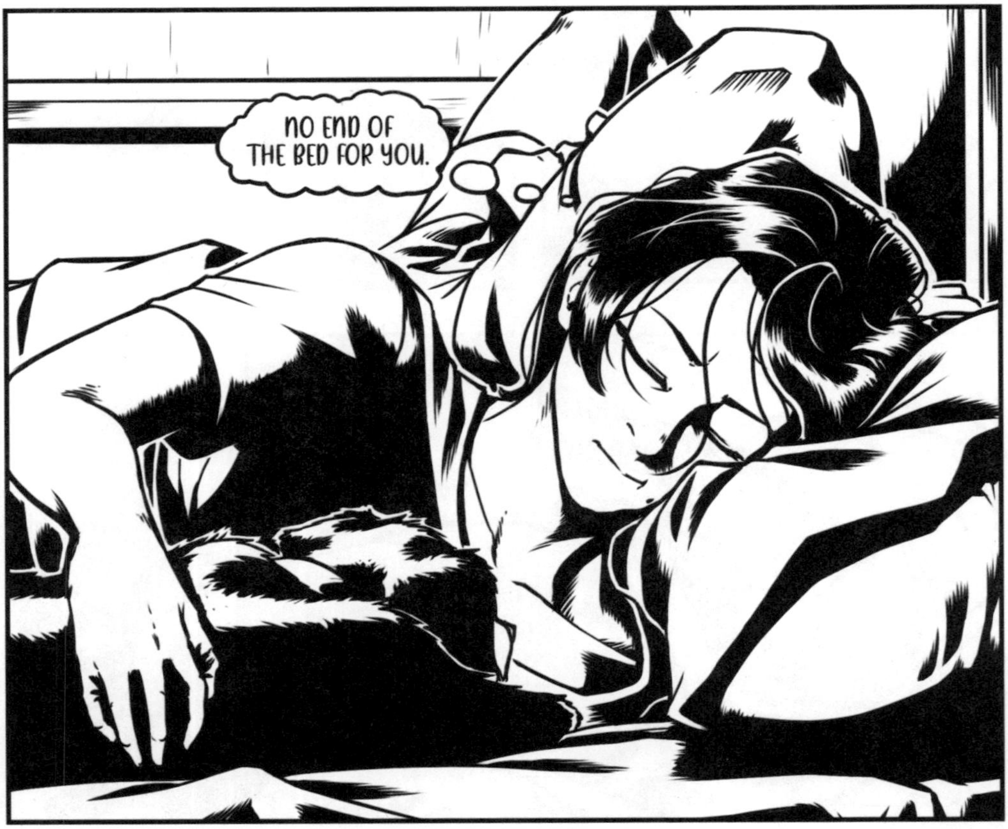
NO END OF THE BED FOR YOU.

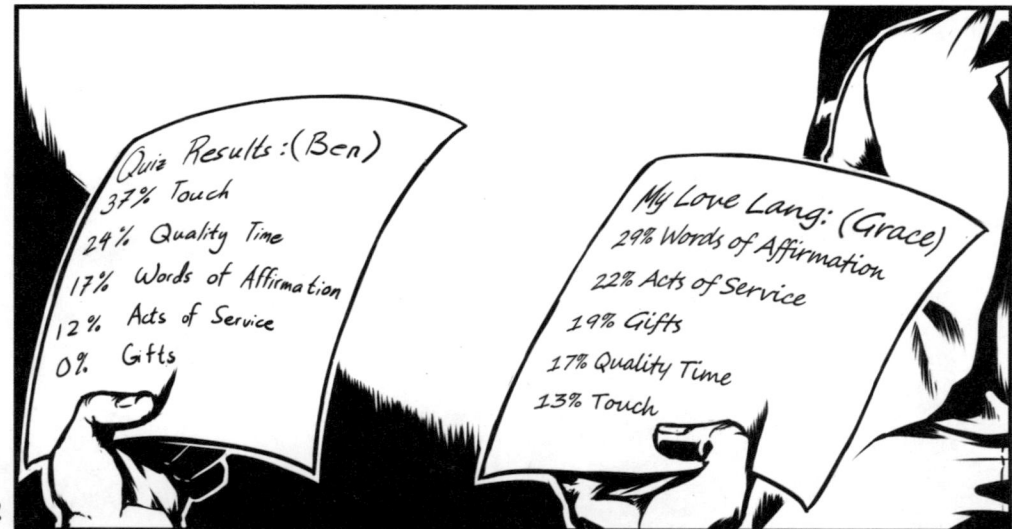

172

174

175

WORDS OF AFFIRMATION.
THANK YOU
I'M PROUD TOF YOU
I VALUE YOU:
SMART
QUIRKY
FUNNY
WITTY
ORGANIZED
A GOOD HEART
GIVING

QUALITY TIME. DOING THINGS TOGETHER.

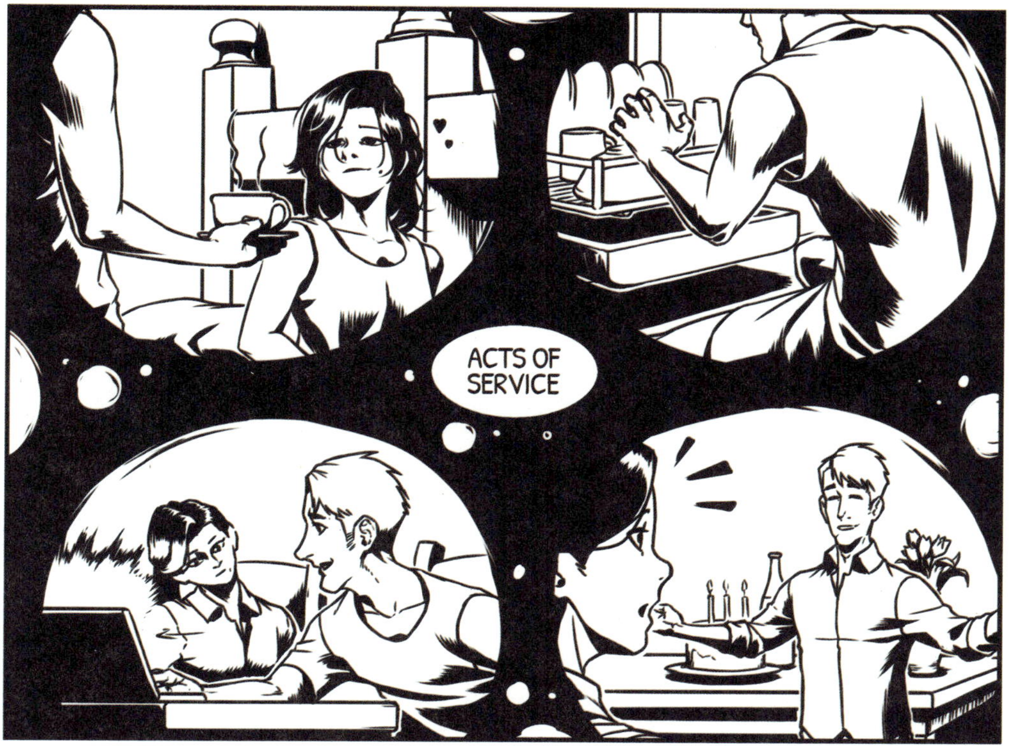
ACTS OF
SERVICE

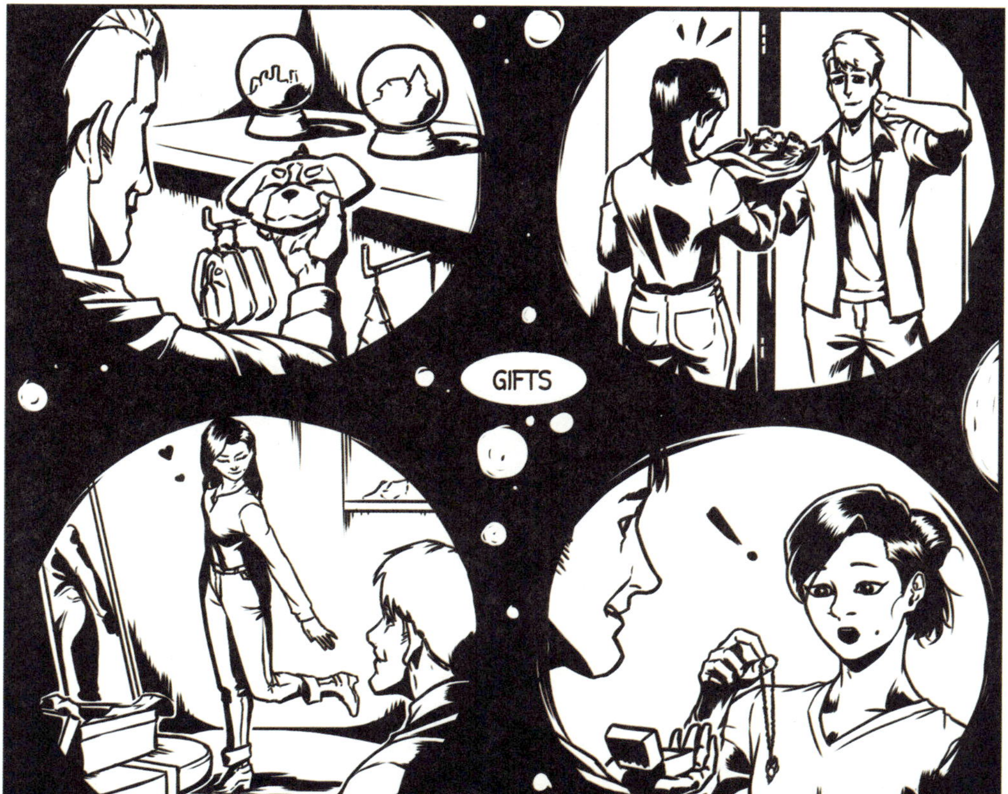
GIFTS

178

EACH OFFER TOPICS TO DISCUSS THAT ARE 3-4 IN DIFFICULTY ON A 1-10 SCALE. THEN DECIDE TOGETHER.

BEN IS QUIET AND DISTANT AT TIMES.

IT'S BECAUSE . . .

GRACE TALKS FOR A LONG TIME.

I DON'T KNOW IF YOU'RE LISTENING.

TOPICS, FOR NOW.

I WISH BEN WOULD DO CHORES WITHOUT BEING REMINDED.

GRACE LIKES TO SHOP MORE THAN I HAVE PATIENCE FOR.

WHICH TOPIC WILL YOU DISCUSS?

181

IMAGINE THERE'S A STRING BETWEEN YOUR MOUTHS. THERE'S A WASHER ON THE STRING.

YOU WANT IT IN THE MIDDLE OVERALL. WHEN YOU TALK, IT PUSHES THE WASHER TOWARD THE OTHER PERSON.

IF YOU TALK LONG, IT SILENCES THE OTHER.

TALK IN SMALL BITES. ASK BEN HOW THAT LOOKS OR SOUNDS TO HIM, OR HOW HE FEELS ABOUT IT.

I'M A VISUAL. GRACE HAS TO GET A SENSE OF THINGS.

USE VISUAL QUESTIONS TO ENGAGE HIM.

183

184

PUT IT INTO PRACTICE

5 LOVE LANGUAGES (LL) IN A NUTSHELL

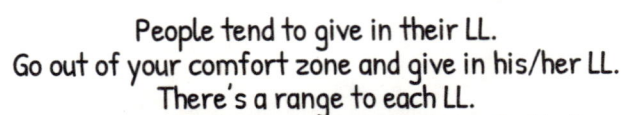

Take the quiz:
https://5lovelanguages.com/quizzes/love-language

People tend to give in their LL.
Go out of your comfort zone and give in his/her LL.
There's a range to each LL.
Experiment, be kind and appreciative of efforts.
LLs won't solve issues; they decrease tension so you can address them.

GOAL IS CENTERED WASHER

Imagine a washer on a string between your mouths.
Talk moves the washer toward your partner.
Speak in short bites and ask questions.
Talking too long silences your partner.
Quieter partner: Use your words!

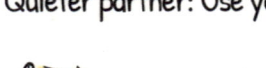

ARE YOU A VISUAL, AUDITORY, OR KINESTHETIC PERSON?

Use language of your partner's style.

How does that . . .

. . . look to you?
. . . sound to you?
. . . feel to you?

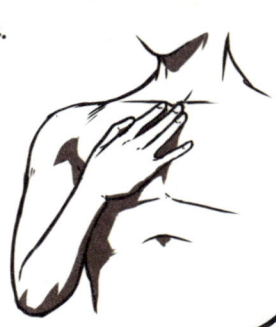

- On page 170, panel 1 and page 171, panel 3: What could Ben have said or done that would have made his feelings understood and have gone over as well as possible for Grace?

'I' statements	Process vs Content	Share how he felt
Was transparent	Used Traffic Lights	All of these

- Look at page 173, panels 1-2: What are Love Languages all about?

- On page 181, panel 5: Which of you talks a lot?
  Which of you talks a little?

- Reflect on your family growing up. Who talked a lot?
  Who talked a little?

- Growing up, what did you learn about talking?

- On page 183, panels 1-3: Describe the Washer tool:

- Also on page 183, panels 3-4 and page 185, panel 1: Are you a Visual, Auditory, or Kinesthetic?

- On page 187, panel 3: Is kindness part of your relationship?   Yes   No

- What do you know about kindness in yourself, and in your family growing up?

TAKEAWAYS

- What are Grace's takeaways from Chapter 6?

- What are Ben's takeaways from Chapter 6?

- What are your takeaways from Chapter 6?

HOMEWORK

YOUR HOMEWORK IS TO TAKE THE 5 LOVE LANGUAGES QUIZ IF YOU HAVEN'T ALREADY. PRACTICE THE WASHER TOOL, FIGURE OUT YOUR MODE OF LEARNING/PROCESSING (VISUAL, AUDITORY, OR KINESTHETIC).

KEEP UP TRAFFIC LIGHTS AND PERSONAL WEATHER REPORTS (FOR THE REST OF YOUR DAYS!)

Chapter 7:

HOW TO BUILD A
BETTER MARRIAGE

Your Relationship is Your Top Priority

HIS SHOULDERS RELAXED.

SINK

Thanks for using my love language.

LEAN

CLASP

WHAT DID WE DO TO MAKE OUR MARRIAGE BETTER THIS WEEK?

WOW, MAYBE IT'S EXACTLY WHAT WE NEED.

GRACE, WHAT'S YOUR SENSE OF YOU TWO BEING EACH OTHER'S PRIORITY?

WHAT DOES THAT EVEN MEAN?

I'M HAVING A HARD TIME GETTING THAT.

SURE DIDN'T SEE IT. BUT THE IMAGE OF THE ROOF MAKES SENSE.

WHAT MATTERS TO ONE OF YOU NEEDS TO BE IMPORTANT TO BOTH OF YOU.

OKAY . . .

YOU'RE SUGGESTING THAT I CHANGE FUNDAMENTALLY...

FEAR OF FAILURE.

FAILURE/POSSIBILITY.

IF IT WORKS, WE COULD BE HAPPIER.

I NEED TO THINK ABOUT IT A LOT.

I'M STRUGGLING TO GET IT. HOW . . . ?

DO OUR CAREERS FALL BY THE WAYSIDE?

YOU HAVE THE CAPACITY TO PRIORITIZE YOUR MARRIAGE AND DO A GOOD JOB AT WORK, TOO.

YOU BELIEVE WE CAN?

ABSOLUTELY. AS WITH ALL THESE TOOLS AND SKILLS, YOU'LL MAKE MISTAKES AND LEARN FROM THEM. THAT'S HUMAN NATURE. BE KIND TO YOURSELF AND EACH OTHER.

IF I'M NOT KIND TO MYSELF, HOW CAN I BE KIND TO BEN?

I HATE MAKING MISTAKES.

MAYBE BECAUSE YOUR PARENTS CRITICIZED?

207

SO YOUR PARENTS CRITICIZING YOU DOESN'T MEAN YOU ARE A MISTAKE?

ONLY ON MY GOOD DAYS.

I THINK I'M STARTING TO GET THIS.

JUST SIT WITH IT FOR A BIT.

CAN WE MOVE ON?

ENOUGH TO DIGEST

UNCOMFORTABLE.

SO I NEED TO TELL GRACE WHEN SOMETHING IS IMPORTANT TO ME AND VICE-VERSA?

YES. IT DOESN'T MEAN THAT IT CAN HAPPEN IMMEDIATELY. IT'S ON THE TABLE TO DISCUSS AND LOOK AT FROM WHAT'S BEST FOR YOUR MARRIAGE.

OKAY, I'M READY TO CHANGE TOPICS.

NOD

WHAT ARE YOUR TAKEAWAYS FROM TODAY?

I NEED TIME TO DIGEST EVERYTHING FROM TODAY.

AGAIN, MY SENSE OF SELF FROM CHILDHOOD IS FLAWED.

PUT IT INTO PRACTICE

YOUR MARRIAGE IS YOUR TOP PRIORITY

This creates emotional security and safety, leading to intimacy.

With each decision ask, "What's best for our marriage?"

What matters to one of you needs to be important to both of you.

You're still you while prioritizing your marriage.

You have the capacity to prioritize your marriage and a do a good job at work, too.

WRITE, DRAW OR HEAR YOUR MARRIAGE HOPES AND CONCERNS ABOUT USING THESE TOOLS

HOPES

CONCERNS

PUT IT INTO PRACTICE

- See pages 195–198: What tools and information have Grace and Ben learned?

  3 Brains   Love Languages   Personal Weather Report

  The value of Feelings   Responding vs Reacting   Washer

  Slowing down   Transparency   Curiosity   Traffic Lights

  Editorializing   Childhood impacts   All of these

- Look at page 201, panel 3: What is the tool that Jo offers?

- On page 202, panel 1: Did you think what Ben and Grace thought?   Yes   No

- On page 202: Why is making your relationship your priority important?

- On page 202, panel 3: How is it implemented?

- How do you feel about making your relationship your top priority?

- See page 206, panel 3: How does Jo's belief in Ben and Grace and the process help them? Write, draw, or think of a song lyric to describe it.

- See page 206, panel 3: Will Grace and Ben make mistakes?   Yes   No

- See page 206, panel 3: What will help?

- Look at page 207, panel 3: What are the two 'animals' in Jo's statement?

  Being a disappointment   AND   Doing something that's disappointing
  to someone else

PUT IT INTO PRACTICE

TAKEAWAYS

- What are Grace's takeaways from Chapter 7?

- What are Ben's takeaways from Chapter 7?

- What are your takeaways from Chapter 7?

HOMEWORK

YOUR HOMEWORK IS ON PAGE 212 AND PAGE 213.

Acknowledgments

IN writing the series *I Do, I Don't: How to Build a Better Marriage*, I set out to incorporate a wide range of psychological teachings from many disparate sources, over many decades, into a useful practical resource to use today and everyday.

Thank you to my many teachers and mentors in the psychotherapeutic community: Abraham Maslow; Virginia Satir; Irv Yalom; Sue Johnson; John and Julie Gottman; and the authors of the attachment assessment.

More Specifically:

Traffic Lights; Washer; Difficulty scale of topics; Green shoots — Kathryn Ford

Attachment Theory — John Bowlby and Mary Ainsworth, et al

Anchor, Island, Wave terms for Attachment Theory; Secure Functioning term — Stan Tatkin

Brain Science — Dan Siegel, Richard Lannon, Chris Sorensen, Thomas Lewis, et al

Competence Chart — William Howell

Saying back what you heard; Accuracy; Giving empathy — Harville Hendrix

The 5 Love Languages — Gary Chapman

Learning Styles — Neil Fleming

Feeling Lists from About.com 2008

Unconscious — Carl Jung

Facial Expressions & Body Language — Rob Fisher

Neuroplasticity — Adolf Meyer, et al

Strange Situation — Mary Ainsworth

Still Face — Ed Tronick

Inevitably one cannot mention many others. I am forever indebted to the wonderful work of countless creative minds in this field, and regret that I was not able to mention them all.

Thank You

MY heartfelt gratitude to: Locke Anderson, my husband (I adore you) and champion; Dallas Middaugh, my first mentor; my incredible artist, Nur Jaffar G. Latip; Holly Brady, who suggested the title; Janis Dolnick and Lynn Meinhardt early readers; Brian Anderson, my CTO; Rob Clough, for his extraordinary wordsmithing and support; John Kilcullen for his vision and help; Woodrow Phoenix, book designer; John Anderson, my publisher.

Many others offered love, support and encouragement throughout the process. I value and appreciate all of you.

About the Author and Artist

Chandrama Anderson, MA, LMFT
(Calif. Lic # MFC 45204.)

Chandrama is a Licensed Marriage and Family Therapist since 2007, and the president of Connect2 Marriage Counseling, Inc. Chandrama combines knowledge from many fields–anything that lights her passion for couples–to help you be your genuine self, find your own voice, and build a better relationship. Her previous career in Silicon Valley included positions at Apple, Stanford University and IDG Books' *For Dummies*. Chandrama has a robust background in speaking and teaching, as well as television appearances.

Chandrama is a wife, mom, sister, and friend. She enjoys reading, hiking, aqua fitness, riding a tandem bike with her husband, watching movies, the 49ers and Giants. Chandrama loves the beach and mountains; nature is her place of restoration.

Nur Jaffar G. Latip, Artist

Nur Jaffar Latip is a talented young Filipino artist, living in Marawi. Trained as an engineer, his true passion lies in his talents as a digital illustrator and cartoonist. His nuanced understanding of character design and gesture, his sophisticated use of color, and his solid storytelling chops mark him as an artist to watch.

Other Books by
Chandrama Anderson, MA, LMFT

Connect2 Personality Mapping:
A Breakthrough Psychotherapy Process Tool for
Understanding Your Clients, Their Families and Their
Relationships
ISBN: 9781461080329
(Connect2 Publishing, 2012)

No U-Turn at Mercy Street:
A Memoir and Resource Guide for Grieving Parents
ISBN: 9781453623602
(Connect2 Publishing, 2010)

A Hard Road:
A Story of Cancer Survival for Patients and Caregivers
ISBN: 9781532794780
(Connect2 Publishing, 2017)

Options for Working with Chandrama

To participate in a US or international *I Do, I Don't* reading group via videoconferencing: www.connect2relate.com

To learn more about current offerings: www.connect2relate.com

For couple or individual adult relationship therapy (California residents only, per licensing requirements): canderson.connect2@gmail.com

For speaking, teaching, or general information: www.connect2relate.com

Please join my email list: www.connect2relate.com

For Peer-only *I Do, I Don't* Reading Groups

To participate in an *I Do, I Don't* reading group of peers, visit: www.connect2relate.com

For Graphic Novel Art or Illustration

For amazing art, contact Nur at: nurjaffarlatip@gmail.com. Please note, Nur is very busy working on the next book in the *I Do, I Don't* series!